# Death

*An Exploration*

Learning to Embrace
Life's Most Feared Mystery

## Loren Mayshark

REDSCORPION
— PRESS —

Library of Congress Control Number: 2016934935
Published by Red Scorpion Press
www.redscorpionpress.com
P.O. Box 289
Bemus Point, New York 14712
Copyright © 2016 by Loren Mayshark

First Printing: March 2016
First Edition: March 2016
ISBN-13: 978-0692651643

# Dedication

*To my father, who has shown me the other side of many things. Without his unique perspectives, I would not have cultivated the nuanced worldview that I have today.*

# Acknowledgements

This book would not have been possible without the love and devotion of my parents. They have shown me that there are many ways to live life and many ways to view death. They have helped me through dark times and to overcome great obstacles. Without their love and affection, I would not have undertaken such a project. Special thanks to my mother, who has doggedly helped me complete this project, along with many others. Thank you also to their partners, Jeannine Miller and Jim McElrath, who encouraged my work and offered valuable opinions and insights. Thanks also to Kevin McElrath, who did important research on the topic and gave me solid feedback on the initial draft.

A special nod to my mentor, Bill Bode. He left us too quickly; his insights were brilliant, his manner light and always humble, particularly given his unique abilities. He taught me a great deal about life, death, and prose.

To Brian "Little Guy" Hudec and Ray Tomasini, who live on in my thoughts and dreams.

In memory of Carl Dominick, a giant of a man, who was always kind to me. I am forever grateful to him for leaving such a fine legacy—a fine family where I can feel included.

In memory of my uncle Thomas Curro, who showered me with love and initiated me into the reality of loss, and James Page Mayshark, Sr., who stands alone as a great pillar of my life. His final gift was showing me what loss and death are. And to Felice Lipari, a man I barely knew in person, but whom I am thankful that I got to know through the magical stories that my amazing grandmother continues to tell. I must acknowledge my luck in having both my grandmothers: Laura Lipari and Walt Mayshark are still in my life to show me other folds of this reality. And I am grateful that my aunt Virginia is here to continue to encourage and support me. She gives me much to strive for and look up to, for every day she is a living testament to the power of love.

A special thanks to editor Keith Miller, who has helped me tighten the prose and simplified the difficult process of publishing my first book.

To Aunt Mary and Uncle Tony, who have always nurtured my being and nourished my writing. To my aunt Vivian, who shares her powerful mind with me. And to my friends and members of my family whom I have not named here but who have been with me every step of the way, for you I am forever grateful. THANK YOU.

# Contents

Introduction                                              3

 I: Living with Death                                     7

II: Why Don't We Die Like Salmon?                        15

III: The Wild Abyss                                       21

IV: Death, Fear, and Ayahuasca                           31

V: Immortality in the Silicon Valley                     37

VI: Steve Jobs: On the Doorstep of Eternity              43

VII: "American Immortal": Oliver Sacks and
       Ezekiel J. Emanuel                                49

VIII: Facing Uncertainty Without Religion               59

IX: Beyond the Final Curtain: Reincarnation
       and the Afterlife                                 67

Conclusion                                               79

# DEATH: AN EXPLORATION

# Introduction

*"Death is like a mirror in which the true meaning of life is reflected."*

—SOGYAL RINPOCHE

When my grandfather, a strong man with hands like meat hooks, died after a long bout with Alzheimer's disease and other physical ailments stemming from a hard life, it was not a surprise. His amazing life had included such hardships as serving in World War II and earning a Purple Heart, and there was an understandable mixture of pain and relief in my family when he made his final exit. Being only seventeen at the time, I was shaken, especially when I saw my father break down in tears as he spoke of their sometimes strained relationship. I felt my father's anguish as he choked out his emotions before our entire family, his friends, and members of the Unitarian church where my grandmother was very active. I did not accompany my family to the morgue; death was weighing too heavily on my mind. I was flooded with emotions and unable to prepare myself for what I imagined would unfold there.

My father smiles when he recounts how they showed the family around the funeral parlor. The family said one last goodbye before my grandfather was placed in the incinerator. As his flesh burned down to the bones, my father told me, they peered curiously at the stove from outside. After some time had passed — whether it was a ten minutes or an hour, my father was not sure — my cousin, a photographer, asked if the mortician could open the door to the furnace so they could peer in at my grandfather's remains and take some pictures. The mortician seemed taken aback by the request and told my cousin that it was the first time he had ever had that request. He said he would open the door for them but added that he wasn't doing her any favors. While they peered into the flames engulfing my grandfather's remains, my cousin opened the shutter a few times.

That moment has been seared into my memory. Just today I looked again at the photo and thought about my grandfather, a six-foot-three standout tight end at Lehigh University, being reduced to ashes. His skeleton was hardly discernible in the flurry of flames. Looking at him in there made me think of fire. My grandfather's spirit, which had once burned so brightly, had long since drifted away. The flames would cease, reducing the mass that was once his body to cold ashes. The earth would still rotate on its axis. My days would continue, and he would only live on in the memories of those left behind. It was hard for me then, but with the separation, the passing of years, and the learning I have done since, it has become easier.

In this book we will take an intellectual journey into death, viewing it from many different angles. Through this endeavor you may encounter aspects of death that you might not have considered. This information can be used by children and people of all ages to better cope with the inevitability of an end to our current earthly existence. I hope that by sharing these insights with you the experience can be as liberating for you as the process has been for me. Thank you for taking the time to read these words.

# CHAPTER I
## Living with Death

*"Men fear death, as children fear to go in the dark; and as that natural fear in children, is increased with tales, so is the other."*
—FRANCIS BACON

My upbringing was very different from that of my peers. Some might say that I grew up in a haunted house, surrounded by death. I grew up with a skeleton in the living room that my father had acquired through some elaborate business deal, involving rooting around in some man's cellar. I looked into the face of death in the living room every day. At first it freaked me out to see someone who had once been alive, like me, but was no longer. However, I went from being scared as a child to occasionally being startled by the skeleton to being curious. I would stare at it and brood on the bones restructured into a cold representation of the human that once was. Although we first thought the deceased person in our living room to be a man, from the hip structure we deduced that she had in fact been an unusually tall woman for her time. We changed her name from William to Willa May.

Willa May was the crown jewel of the dead that populated our house. The walls were festooned with mummified cats, turtle shells, and skulls of various animals. Pig embryos in jars sat on the windowsill. In the freezer there were birds and reptiles in various stages of decomposition. Perhaps because of this upbringing that some might call macabre, I have always had what seems to be an unusual fascination with the final destination. I have never been obsessed with death, but I have fantasized about it, gone through the death of loved ones, and in dreams have faced my own.

Although dealing with death as a child was confusing, I experienced death on many levels. Most notable was the loss of my great-uncle Tom, with whom I was very close. He was an intelligent man with a legendary background in athletics and business. Even though he was advanced in years, we would wrestle on

the floor when I was four or five. He was always gener-
ous with his time and went out of his way to give me
little extras, including treats and the kind of attention
that endears a child to an older relative. His passing
when I was only seven gave me a new perspective on
death. It was an uneasy initiation to the lifelong pain
of losing those we love. It was hard for me to understand that I would never see him again.

Having Willa May in the house and being surrounded by artifacts from dead animals, combined
with experiencing the loss of someone so important, I
was forced to contemplate death. This compelled me
to consider the vestiges of death; the remains of beings
that had once existed but were no longer alive.

Over the years I have lost good friends and rela-
tives and, as I assume nearly everyone has, I have con-
tinued to ponder what death means. One important
result of this introspection: I have tried to find a
deeper meaning behind what it means to be alive.
Death is one of the only certainties in life. We live in a
world of dualities: hot and cold, male and female,
young and old, etc. So if there is life, then logically
there must be the opposite.

As far as we know, we are the only species that

analyzes the phenomenon of death. Reliving an imagined death over and again without actually experiencing death can compound the suffering. But only those who can appreciate death for what it is and begin to see the possibilities in it are able to find some relief from the dark shadow that this inevitability seems to cast. Why don't more people approach it, as many of our visionaries have, as a release? Those who were able to see death as more than some diabolical riddle or an end to everything seem to lead fuller lives. Consider this quote from Wolfgang Amadeus Mozart:

> As death, when we come to consider it closely, is the true goal of our existence, I have formed during the last few years such close relations with this best and truest friend of mankind, that his image is not only no longer terrifying to me, but is indeed very soothing and consoling! And I thank my God for graciously granting me the opportunity (you know what I mean) of learning that death is the key which unlocks the door to our true happiness.[1]

But it seems that our society moves to a different beat than Mozart did. The subject of death becomes even more complex when we consider the role of vio-

---

[1] Karol Berger, *Bach's Cycle, Mozart's Arrow: An Essay on the Origins of Musical Modernity.* (Berkley and Los Angeles: University of California Press, 2008), 190.

lence in our society, because death is often the product of extreme violence. Brutality seems omnipresent, from the increasingly gory movies and television shows to mass shootings that plague the United States. Almost every week, it seems, there is another mass shooting. The obsession people have with murder mysteries and serial killers is insatiable. We also seem to have an unquenchable desire for tales of undead monsters, specifically vampires and zombies. What does this say about death and our quality of life?

*"The first breath is the beginning of death."*

—THOMAS FULLER

We grow from babies to adults, and our bodies and minds go through many changes. After passing through the awkward crucible of adolescence we amble into adulthood, without the rites many primal societies retain to signify reaching womanhood or manhood. After we wax strong, with most raising families and nurturing careers, there comes a time when we start to lose things: memories, muscle mass, thoughts, and abilities. We hit the pinnacle and enter the decline. Slowly, things we took for granted in our youth are gone or don't work the same. Eventually, as Warren Zevon said as he was aging, "Your shit's fucked up... The shit that used to work / It won't work now."[2] During this process of regression we start to become children again, not as sure on our feet, in need of the care of others—vulnerable. With many older people, a jovial innocence returns that can be only seen in the smile of a child. The process of returning to the place from where we came, which poet Harold Brodkey referred to as "wild darkness," can be unsettling, but it is a road we all must walk. This is the cycle of life that those who make it to old age experience in its entirety. But we do not forget that death happens at all ages and is experienced by all people.

In the words of my father (speculating after copious bourbon consumption): "You return to the best place you've ever been . . . when you die, you go back to the womb and you come out kicking and screaming because it was so wonderful and you hate to leave." I later realized that this notion was similar to the words of the philosopher Arthur Schopenhauer, who contended that "after your death you will be what you were before your birth." This point of view takes the

---

[2] Warren Zevon, "Warren Zevon Lyrics," *Metro Lyrics*, n.d., accessed November 6, 2015, http://www.metrolyrics.com/my-shits-fucked-up-lyrics-warren-zevon.html.

ability to look beyond our learned experiences to something greater; perhaps, as Carl Jung speculated, to a collective unconscious, which is something that we are connected to and is bigger than ourselves.

How can we be so certain that death is something to be feared? Is there any other reason for this than mystery? Plato reminds us of a simple truth that has not changed in thousands of years: "To fear death, gentlemen, is no other than to think oneself wise when one is not, to think one knows what one does not know. No one knows whether death may not be the greatest of all blessings for a man, yet men fear it as if they knew that it is the greatest of evils. And surely it is the most blameworthy ignorance to believe that one knows what one does not know." Heeding the words of Plato, I recall that almost nothing is certain. But these thoughts are even more powerful when considered alongside this quote by neurologist Oliver Sacks: "There will be no one like us when we are gone, but then there is no one like anyone else, ever. When people die, they cannot be replaced. They leave holes that cannot be filled, for it is the fate—the genetic and neural fate—of every human being to be a unique individual, to find his own path, to live his own life, to die his own death."[3]

As I have grown from child to adult, death has appeared to me in many forms. Experiencing death has dragged me into emotional pits and has also compelled me to deep contemplation. This journey has filled me with wonderment as well as remorse. In the following chapters we will look at death from many other perspectives, which I hope will build to a whole greater than the sum of its parts.

3. Oliver Sacks, "Oliver Sacks on Learning He Has Terminal Cancer," *The New York Times*, February 19, 2015, accessed August 5, 2015, http://www.nytimes.com/2015/02/19/opinion/oliver-sacks-on-learning-he-has-terminal-cancer.html.

## CHAPTER II
# Why Don't We Die Like Salmon?

*"That which is so universal as death must be a benefit."*

—FRIEDRICH VON SCHILLER

I have often thought about the cycle of our lives and how it fits into the broader cycles of nature. Many creatures have cyclical spawning migrations, which lead them back to the place of their birth, where they will give life to the next generation. Human beings are not beholden to such patterns, which makes the nature of our birth, life, and death cycles different from those of many other creatures. Although many of us have children, it is not an imperative. It seems that much of our lives are spent searching for meaning rather than being tethered to an innate urge to fulfill a natural pilgrimage to reproduction and death. Although reproduction has a strong presence in our lives, it is not as inextricably linked to death as it is for other species. We are part of the animal kingdom but our evolution has placed us in a different rhythm. This makes us consider how we are linked to the greater picture.

Eva Saulitis is a marine biologist and writer who has deeply considered these questions, and her experiences give her a unique perspective on life and death. Every September for twenty-six years, Saulitis visited the same scene of black humpback salmon fighting their way upstream to spawn and die. Each year was a unique variation of a gory slaughter, with salmon ripped apart by bears, carried to death in the talons of bald eagles, or smashed against rocks by currents and members of their own species. Propelled by a mysterious, innate sense of duty, the salmon would give their utmost in order to birth a new generation. They were destined to spawn new life or feed the fire burning in the stomachs of the predators that flourished on their flesh.

Are the salmon aware of their impending doom? Do they, like humans, have to live with the central existential angst, stemming from the fact that one day they would cease to be? It is important to recognize that, in one way or another, all creatures are beholden to death.

The salmon scene in Saulitis's twenty-sixth year of observation was very different in her perception than it had been before, for she had been recently diagnosed with metastatic breast cancer, a terminal condition. In her most recent bout with the disease she'd had surgery as part of a six-day stint in the hospital where she endured untold pain and the difficulty of being hooked to various machines. This led her to observe: "In the hospital, I learned to fear something more than death: existence dependent upon technology, machines, sterile procedures, hoses, pumps, chemicals easing one kind of pain only to feed a psychic other. Existence apart from dirt, mud, muck, wind gust, crow caw, fishy orca breath, bog musk, deer track, rain squall, bear scat." She continues, explaining her observation by offering a philosophical reality with far reaching dimensions: "The whole ordeal was a necessary palliation, a stint of suffering to grant me long-term physical freedom. And yet it smacked of the way people too often spend their last days alive, and it really scared me."[4]

[4] Eva Saulitis, "Cancer: Into the Wild Darkness," *The Week*, accessed August 5, 2015, http://theweek.com/articles/446879/cancer-into-wild-darkness.

We can't say with certainty that we are the only species that is aware of its own death. But there are no experts on what lies beyond the boundaries of the living world. There are people who have had near-death experiences and can recount, in great detail, what they believe they have seen beyond the curtain. As Saulitis says in her article "Into the Wild Darkness," we are still in the dark because "we know more about the universe and the mind of an octopus than we do about death's true nature. Only that it is terrible and inescapable, and it is wild."

Here it is important to remember a fact that was not mentioned in Saulitis's article about this natural deadly dance with eternity. It is the law of the conservation of energy: energy cannot be created or destroyed. As far as we know, all the energy that exists in the universe always has been and as far as we can tell always will be, so perhaps we do not die; we simply lose our human bodies and change form.

In the United States, we often prolong people's lives far beyond the point that they can function in a dignified way. We force people to live as human puddles, hooked into tubes feeding them medications that are imperative to survival, slowly ebbing away until eventually passing over to the other side. About 32 percent of the U.S. Medicare budget goes to end-of-life care.[5] To wither away in a hospital bed jammed full of tubes, needles, and chemicals does not do justice to the dignity of the person who was once a fully functioning human being.

Saulitis eloquently lights on this uncomfortable truth as she meditates on her own condition and how different it is from the salmons' last stand. She says that "facing death in a death-phobic culture is lonely. But in wild places like Prince William Sound or the woods and sloughs behind my house, it is different. The salmon dying in their stream tell me I am not alone. The evidence is everywhere: in the skull of an immature eagle I found in the woods; in the bones of a moose in the gully below my house; in the corpse of a wasp on the windowsill; in the fall of a birch leaf from its branch. These things tell me death is true, right, graceful; not tragic, not failure, not defeat."[6]

There is something so natural about death because it is all around us; every living organism has to dance with death. In the end Saulitis eloquently cap-

---

[5] "End of Life Care," *Dartmouth Atlas of Medical Care*, accessed August 18, 2015, http://www.dartmouthatlas.org/keyissues/issue.aspx?con=2944.

[6] Saulitis, "Cancer: Into the Wild Darkness."

tures this truth: "Death is nature. Nature is far from over. In the end, the gore at the creek comforts more than it appalls. In the end—I must believe it—just like a salmon, I will know how to die, and though I die, though I lose my life, nature wins. Nature endures. It is strange, and it is hard, but it's comfort, and I'll take it."[7]

I have long meditated on death's role in the cycles of nature. I have often contemplated the mysterious interior lives of animals. Why do salmon return to their birth to spawn a new generation and end their own lives? Why are these choices made? Why is there so little deviation within other species, in comparison to the myriad of ways our species chooses to live? How far has our society removed us from the rhythms of the natural world? It seems to me that contemplation is often most mystical when it is enveloped in nature, leading to deeper insights. With heightened understanding one comes to see death as part of the lifecycle; an experience we all share. From this one can glean some solace.

[7] Saulitis, "Cancer: Into the Wild Darkness."

# CHAPTER III
# The Wild Abyss

*"Let the children walk with Nature, let them see the beautiful blendings and communions of death and life, their joyous inseparable unity as taught in woods and meadows, plains and mountains and streams of our blessed star, and they will learn that death is stingless indeed, and as beautiful as life."*

—JOHN MUIR

Many brilliant people have examined death, with very different outcomes. Some of the most admirable and courageous faced death with open eyes; when they felt it was time they did not hesitate. Virginia Woolf walked into the River Ouse with stones in her pockets. She exemplifies people who had a connection to nature and in a real and symbolic way revisited it in their final moment.

The connection between death and nature is

deep. They share many intriguing aspects, including the inherent mystery. Some of those willing to immerse themselves in nature seem compelled to walk at the edge of the precipice of the great beyond.

*Into the Wild* follows the life of a wiry young adventurer named Chris McCandless who lived his life close to the edge and then had it slip away in the Alaskan wilderness at the age of twenty-four. He was a naturalist and adventurer who greatly respected several notable American naturalist writers, including Henry David Thoreau and Jack London. He was one of the many young men who seem to be most at home away from the hullabaloo of life within society, cloaked in the simplistic beauty of the natural world. He did it in a way that was extreme to the point that he endured untold discomforts and flirted with death until his untimely demise. He was out of step with society, eschewing anything beyond utter necessities. At an early point in his journey he abandoned his car and set his last $123 on fire. He wished to live a life of freedom, often teetering on the edge.

The author of *Into the Wild*, John Krakauer, sees many parallels between McCandless and a young adventurer named Everett Ruess, who spent much of his life wandering the country in search of beauty. Wallace Stegner, who studied Ruess's life and became so fascinated with the young man that he dedicated a number of works to him, said that he was "a callow romantic, an adolescent esthete, an atavistic wanderer of the wastelands."[8] Ruess, who died in 1934 at the age of twenty, seemed to take some pleasure in the discomfort of his wild lifestyle. He documented numerous scrapes with death, such as tangling with poisonous snakes and nearly avoiding crippling falls from crumbling cliffs. Once a severe case of poison ivy debilitated him while he was apparently starving, and he wrote: "For two days I couldn't tell whether I was dead or alive. I writhed and twisted in the heat, with swarms of ants and flies crawling over me, while the poison oozed and crusted on my face and arms and back. I ate nothing—there was nothing to do but suffer philosophically . . ."[9] Reading about Ruess and McCandless makes them sound almost masochistic in their relationships with pain and death.

This raises the consideration of three alluring qualities that death shares with raw nature, and that compels human beings to do severe things; things

---

[8] Jon Krakauer, *Into the Wild*, (New York: Anchor Books, 1996), 90.
[9] Ibid., 93.

some might consider crazy: the mystery, the power, and the strange beauty. Although the finality of death is constantly on display in the natural world, nature itself continues while all the organisms that are part of nature must meet their demise.

The young Ruess seems unshaken and somewhat enchanted by this inevitability. As he stated in one of his letters: "I have been thinking more and more that I shall always be a lone wanderer of the wilderness. God, how the trail lures me. You cannot comprehend its resistless fascination for me. After all the lone trail is the best . . . I'll never stop wandering. And when the time comes to die, I'll find the wildest, loneliest, most desolate spot there is."[10]

It is this reckless abandon of these young men that separated them from most people, placing them closer to the abyss. This was something that Krakauer himself understood because he, as an avid climber, undertook many ill-conceived adventures that placed him uncomfortably close to death, including a harrowing trip to climb the Devil's Thumb in Alaska, which he recounts in the book. As he reflects on the event, eighteen years later, he realizes that he "suffered

---

[10] Krakauer, 91.

from hubris, perhaps, and an appalling innocence, certainly," but noted that he "wasn't suicidal." He came to understand that at that point in his young life, "death remained as abstract a concept as non-Euclidean geometry or marriage. I didn't yet appreciate its terrible finality or the havoc it could wreak on those who'd entrusted the deceased with their hearts. I was stirred by the dark mystery of mortality. I couldn't resist stealing up to the edge of doom and peering over the brink. The hint of what was concealed in those shadows terrified me, but I caught sight of something in the glimpse, some forbidden and elemental riddle that was no less compelling than the sweet, hidden petals of a woman's sex." Interestingly, he believes that he shared the same fascination with death that McCandless did, but for Krakauer it was a passion that ended with curiosity. He writes: "In my case—and, I believe, in the case of Chris McCandless—that was a very different thing from wanting to die."[11]

There are many similarities between aesthetically entranced adventurers like Ruess and McCandless and extreme athletes. In one of his final interviews before an abrupt ending to an extraordinary life, extreme ath-

[11] Krakauer, 155–56.

lete Dean Potter tried to answer interviewer Joe O'Connor's question regarding what it was like to jump off a cliff in a wingsuit and glide through the air, seconds before one has to deploy a parachute or die. The essence of it, said Potter, is that "you are engaged in beauty, and the thing that really heightens our awareness even beyond danger is beauty." Later in the interview he explains how it becomes an obsession: "The hook are these heightened states that we get, way beyond perception, with the intensity of the danger, and the position and the beauty of these powerful places." But then again, we must fear death in order to survive, both as individuals and as a species. If we didn't, we would kill ourselves as soon as the going got rough.[12]

How do daredevils like Potter view death? Is the ability to stare death in the face something that we lose with age? At forty-two, Potter admitted that he was striving to find more balance in his approach to these death-defying endeavors. He did add that his thinking was influenced by his fallen comrades: "In some ways, I am haunted, and I have the thoughts of

[12] Joe O'Connor, "One of Dean S. Potter's Final Interviews: 'Every Death Has a Lesson,'" *National Post*, accessed August 5, 2015, http://news.nationalpost.com/news/world/extreme-athlete-dean-s-potter-dies-during-failed-wingsuit-flight-in-yosemite-which-has-long-banned-the-practice.

my many, many friends who have passed. But I still have this need, because this is who I am." He then explained that he had become philosophical about the many tragic endings of his friends who were compelled by similar needs: "As sad as it is to lose somebody, and it is devastating but, for instance, every death has a lesson. . . . After a death, emotionally, I am devastated, but also enlivened by the spirit of the fallen brother."[13]

There is an old Irish proverb that states: "Danger and delight grow from the same stalk."[14] Many who dance too closely to the beautiful flame of life are burned. They seek a cleansing release from the dullness of everyday life. But that lulls many into a sleepwalking condition. They immerse themselves in extreme communion with nature or pour adrenaline into their bodies by participating in extreme sports that leave little margin for error. The intensity of having to concentrate fully or have everything one has ever known slip away in a moment creates a sensation of awareness and being alive that can be addictive. Without the specter of death, the ultimate danger, this would not be the case.

[13] O'Connor.
[14] "The Quotations Page," accessed November 6, 2015, http://www.quotationspage.com/quote/34492.html.

Those who have extreme relationships with nature and thrive on death-defying feats have long fascinated me. Are they closer to understanding the mystery of life, and therefore death, because they spin near the edge? They seem to be able to crawl closer to the mysterious wild nexus that envelops everything. Are they rewarded with deep insights? It seems reasonable that, on a certain level, they are addicted to adrenaline and beauty. Although I think there is truth to this insight, it often goes deeper than that. On the whole, this process of drawing nearer seems to continuously intoxicate them, but to call it pure addiction is too simple. Part of this infatuation with nature and peril may lie deep within all of us.

Does each of us flirt with danger and death to varying degrees? Or does fear paralyze some so much that they dare not glance at the edge of the void. For many years I have, often deliberately but sometimes by chance, enjoyed dancing at the edge in the form of rugged travel or reckless risk-taking. Also, I have occasionally participated in meditation in various forms, from sitting quietly in nature to breathing alone in a room devoid of distractions, perhaps trying in my own private way to touch some universal mystery beyond life. This has sometimes led me to wonder where that dangerous and intriguing boundary is, and how deeply we can probe without hazarding our demise.

# CHAPTER IV
## Death, Fear, and Ayahuasca

*"The fear of death follows from the fear of life. A man who lives fully is prepared to die at any time."*

—MARK TWAIN

Fear is a constant theme in our lives. Certain animals, and humans who live like animals, spend their lives gripped by fear. To a great extent, healing is about releasing fears.

The fear of death is one of the most central in the human existence. But living a full life means not being dictated by fear. In the jungles of South America there is a ritual that many say is both deathlike and amazingly liberating for numerous people who have experienced the journey. It is the ritual of drinking ayahuasca, a brew made primarily from the *Banisteriopsis caapi* vine, with a shaman. To drink ayahuasca and embark upon a vision quest is a courageous choice. The influence of the plant mixture can be terrifyingly real and can harshly address the deepest fears and inadequacies of the participant. The connections between death and ayahuasca are deep, as evidenced by the etymology of the word. Jay Griffiths, who had a fascinating experience with ayahuasca in the jungles of South America, explains: "*Aya* means, in the Quechua language, spirit or ancestor or dead person, while *huasca* means vine or rope. It is thus sometimes known as the vine of the dead, because shamans say it puts you in touch with the ancestors, and through it they can communicate with the spirit world. (The name is perhaps influenced by the fact that drinking it can make you feel as if you are dying.)"[15]

Jay Griffiths chronicled her time spent with the Aguaruna, an Amazonian tribe that uses ayahuasca, in her book *Wild: An Elemental Journey*. The Aguaruna have an interesting take on fear gained through their use of ayahuasca. The fear of death, which is the most terrifying aspect to many people, is not a major concern of the Aguaruna. They see death as "crossing to

---

[15] Jay Griffiths, *Wild: An Elemental Journey*, (New York: Jeremy P. Tarcher/Penguin, 2006), 10.

the other side."[16] This crossing to the mysterious side of existence, beyond life, is likened by the tribesmen to the act of crossing a river. Through experience with ayahuasca some of the mystery of death is removed, allowing the participants to gain a greater sense of what death means to life.

Many depressives I have met are paradoxically terrified of death. One would expect that people living with profound sadness would inevitably seek a release from their gloomy perceptions of life and its torments. Some take the ultimate step of ending their own lives, while others suffer through the grayness of chronic depression. Others seek cures through medications. A few turn to hallucinogenic cures like ayahuasca out of desperation, and many depressives who have tried the plant mixture to cure their illness have found startling results. One of the most astonishing transformations was that of Kira Salak, a freelance journalist who documented how ayahuasca cured her of lifelong de-pression.[17] After taking part in several ayahuasca cere-monies with a shaman, she wrote: "Physical and psy-chological ailments that had long burdened me— anxiety disorders, OCD, migraines, knee joint pain,

---

[16] Griffiths, 18.
[17] Kira Salak. *Kira Salak*, 2015, accessed November 6, 2015, http://www.kirasalak.com/.

PTSD, etc.—vanished one after the next and never resurfaced." She jubilantly describes her transformation in this passage:

> It was as if a water-logged wool overcoat had been removed from my shoulders. There was a tangible, visceral feeling of release. I noticed that the nature of my thoughts had completely changed. There were no more morbid, incessant desires to die. Gone was the 'suicidal ideation' that had made joy seem impossible for me, and made my life feel like some kind of punishment. I actually woke up in that hut in the jungle of Peru desiring only to live. Wanting to live. Feeling hope for the first time in my life. It was, without a doubt, miraculous.[18]

Such glowing praise for a hallucinogenic plant may seem strange, but many people have commented on the brew's transformative powers. Padmani, a yoga teacher and spiritual seeker, observes: "Ayahuasca and other plant medicines have the ability to reunite human consciousness with natural and supernatural rhythms. Taken with the correct intention, they can help catalyze a profound shift in our all-too-limited take on things. With the radical deepening and broad-

---

[18] Salak.

34

ening of perspective comes a new brand of happiness—the real stuff that lasts."[19]

Paradoxically, death is inextricably linked to life, yet we know so little about it. A willingness to explore meditation and the use of hallucinogens, specifically ayahuasca, allows us to have greater insights into these "natural and supernatural rhythms." This insight permits the individual to gain a better grasp of seemingly unknowable themes such as eternity. When we ponder the vastness of the universe and eternity, we are closer to understanding the role of death in the mysterious life we are all experiencing. Through these realizations, greater acceptance of the inevitability of death positions us to be happier in our lives. After my journey through these ideas I feel strongly that happiness and a deeper understanding of death are linked phenomena that offer a fuller existence.

[19] Padmani, "Insects, Yoga, and Ayahuasca," in *Toward 2012: Perspectives on the Next Age*, eds. Daniel Pinchbeck and Ken Jordan, (New York: Jeremy P. Tarcher/Penguin, 2008), 112.

# CHAPTER V
# Immortality in the Silicon Valley

Immortality has captured the human imagination since the first glimmer of life. In a world of dualities, if there is mortality, then there must be immortality. The written record is filled with stories of immortal gods and the legends of immortal beings. In the modern day the quest for immortality has taken on new dimensions. This newest incarnation of the immortal quest is led by the wealthy members of technology community who no longer see immortality as an abstract concept. Rather, immortality has become something that is tangible. Some, like Ray Kurzweil, see it as inevitability.

Kurzweil, an inventor who is considered by some to be the modern equivalent of Thomas Edison, is in his late sixties yet believes that he has a good chance of avoiding death. To Kurzweil, death is more pliable than it may seem to the average person. He explains in an interview with the *Wall Street Journal* that people have a tendency to anticipate "linear" change. This, Kurzweil explains, is why people have trouble understanding the "accelerating exponential" transformation that is at the heart of information technology. Like other anti-death zealots in the technological world, he explains that science and technology will supply the answers. Kurzweil asserts that by the 2030s, "we'll be putting millions of nanobots inside our bodies to augment our immune system, to basically wipe out disease. One scientist cured Type I diabetes in rats with a blood-cell-size device already."[20] Furthermore, he believes that by the 2050s these microscopic nano-

---

[20] Andrew Goldman, "Ray Kurzweil Says We're Going to Live Forever," *The New York Times*, January 25, 2013, accessed August 5, 2015, http://www.nytimes.com/2013/01/27/magazine/ray-kurzweil-says-were-going-to-live-forever.html.

bots could be used to create an entire virtual body.

In fact, besides working on his own immortality, Kurzweil has a project to reproduce his father, a brilliant composer who died when Kurzweil was only twenty-two, in a virtual form. He would use leftover pictures and personal effects to render a version of his father so that he could interact with him. But he insists that his father would not be a test-tube baby that he would hang out with, Benjamin Button-style. Rather, it would be a virtual version of his old man that would be, in the words of interviewer Holman W. Jenkins, Jr., "an avatar more like his father than his father ever was—exactly the father Mr. Kurzweil remembers." When asked about his father in a *New York Times* interview, Kurzweil stated: "By 2029, computers will have emotional intelligence and be convincing as people. This implies that these are people with volition just like you and I, not just games that you turn off. Is it my father? You could argue that it's a simulation. But it's not something you can play with." This is hard to imagine, but he believes this new era is rapidly approaching.[21]

Kurzweil may be reaching beyond anything hu-

---

[21] Goldman.

mans have ever thought possible, but he is not alone. Peter Thiel, a cofounder of PayPal, who made a king's ransom selling the company to eBay, is worth upwards of $2 billion. Like other technocrats obsessed with eluding death, Thiel has donated millions to scientists working on technologies that will extend lives, perhaps forever. "I've always had this really strong sense that death was a terrible, terrible thing," Theil reflects. "I think that's somewhat unusual. Most people end up compartmentalizing, and they are in some weird mode of denial and acceptance about death, but they both have the result of making you very passive. I prefer to fight it."[22]

Not everyone agrees with Thiel and Kurzweil. Other notable thinkers do not necessarily celebrate death, but they accept it. Francis Fukuyama, who served on the President's Council on Bioethics, sees death as essential. He says that without death despots would hold on to their oppressive regimes for hundreds of years and it would reduce people's ability to adapt and ultimately survive as a species. He sees the quest to avoid an end to life as negative for humanity,

[22] Ariana Eunjung Cha, "How Silicon Valley's Billionaires Are Trying to Defy Death," *The Week*, May 3, 2015, accessed August 20, 2015, http://theweek.com/articles/552604/how-silicon-valleys-billionaires-are-trying-defy-death.

saying: "I think that research into life extension is going to end up being a big social disaster. Extending the average human life span is a great example of something that is individually desirable by almost everyone but collectively not a good thing. For evolutionary reasons, there is a good reason why we die when we do."[23]

Anyone who has been around long enough realizes that life is not all cream puffs and magic elixirs; it is fraught with pain, discomfort, injustice, and tragedy. As Lucan once surmised "The gods conceal from men the happiness of death, that they may endure life." So are the gods of Silicon Valley missing something essential about death? Steve Jobs may have had a similar background to some of Silicon Valley's aspiring immortals, but he has a very different take on life and death. In the next chapter, we'll look at his views.

The idea of immortality seems exhausting to me. To think of being trapped inside this body, which dwindles a little more each year, is not encouraging. Death is a welcome exit. Without death there would be no urgency and I would not feel compelled to create projects like this book. As a matter of fact, this

---

[23] Cha.

book would be irrelevant without death. As we move forward through time there is some reassurance in the fact that we are all moving together toward something we are each bound to, for no one escapes death. The scary part is the pain of death and thinking about what lies behind the curtain. Nobody knows for sure...

# CHAPTER VI

## Steve Jobs:

## On the Doorstep of Eternity

*"Death is the golden key that opens the palace of eternity."*

—JOHN MILTON

The life of Steve Jobs has been studied by millions of people who are fascinated by the man who was instrumental in countless innovations and is perhaps best known for his crowning achievement, cofounding Apple. The company had this to say as a tribute to their fallen visionary: "Steve's brilliance, passion and energy were the source of countless innovations that enrich and improve all our lives.... The world is immeasurably better because of Steve."[24]

The most comprehensive account of Jobs's life

---

[24] Dominic Rushe, "Steve Jobs, Apple Co-Founder, Dies at 56," *The Guardian*, October 5, 2011, accessed August 5, 2015, http://www.theguardian.com/technology/2011/oct/06/steve-jobs-apple-cofounder-dies.

came from his biographer, Walter Isaacson, who is credited with giving a full account of a man who certainly had his faults, including taking credit for his colleagues' ideas, demeaning his workers, and illegally parking in handicapped spaces. However, he was carefully studied by both admirers and detractors, who were eager to learn the secret of the success that allowed him to amass an estimated $8.3 billion. But Jobs was quick to dismiss his wealth, stating, "Being the richest man in the cemetery doesn't matter to me.... Going to bed at night saying we've done something wonderful . . . that's what matters to me."[25]

He was revered, even by his rivals. As his greatest competitor, Bill Gates, once said, "The world rarely sees someone who has had the profound impact Steve has had, the effects of which will be felt for many generations to come."[26] Many people have spent years studying the life of Steve Jobs, but an important and often overlooked aspect of his life, and something he clearly thought deeply about, was his death. Jobs had a publicly chronicled bout with cancer, which he lost at

[25] Rushe.

[26] Yukari Iwatani Kane and Geoffrey A. Fowler, "Steven Paul Jobs, 1955-2011," *The Wall Street Journal*, October 6, 2011, accessed August 5, 2015, http://www.wsj.com/articles/SB10001424052702303044780-4576410753210811910.

the age of fifty-six.

Jobs obviously contemplated where he was going, and that consideration reinforced the determination with which he lived. His sister, writer Mona Simpson, recalls what she describes as "three distinct periods" of Steve's life: "His full life. His illness. His dying."[27]

Jobs, who had an interest in Eastern religions, had gained a deeper insight into death than the average person. This insight seems to have contributed to his ability to live an extraordinary life and harness his powers to implement his unique vision. Jobs once called death "very likely the single best invention of life."[28] Not only did Jobs get better at many facets of his life; he may have gained a unique perspective on what death is and how to meet it. His sister was in the room with Jobs during his final hours, and she commented: "His breathing changed. It became severe, deliberate, and purposeful. I could feel him counting his steps again, pushing farther than before.... He was working at this, too. Death didn't happen to Steve, he achieved it."[29]

---

[27] Mona Simpson, "A Sister's Eulogy for Steve Jobs," *The New York Times*, October 30, 2011, accessed August 5, 2015, http://www.nytimes.com/2011/10/30/opinion/mona-simpsons-eulogy-for-steve-jobs.html.

[28] Jones, Sam. "Steve Jobs's Last Words: 'Oh Wow. Oh Wow. Oh Wow,'" *The Guardian*, October 31, 2011, accessed August 5, 2015, http://www.theguardian.com/technology/2011/oct/31/steve-jobs-last-words.

[29] Simpson.

The thought of achieving one's own death is somewhat strange. In our modern age it is not normal to think of it as a crown or, as Joseph Campbell called it, "the ornament of life."[30] To so many, the Reaper is coming to take, to deliver only the blackness of finality, the omega to the alpha of life. But Jobs did offer one last note in this regard. His sister recalls that when he was saying his farewells and telling her how he was sorry that they would not grow old together as they had planned, he said "he was going to a better place." These are the words of a man who knows that he is facing the unknown. But Jobs stoically told this to his loved ones to alleviate their worries. In the end, he looked at his family and then "over their shoulders past them" as he uttered his final words: "Oh Wow. Oh Wow. Oh Wow."[31]

Mona Simpson remembers how his loved ones "watched his life compress into a smaller circle." But she marveled that what she "learned from his illness, was how much was still left after so much had been taken away." There was something special about how Jobs saw the world, which allowed him to do amazing

[30] *Mythos, Vol. 2: The Shaping of Our Mythic Tradition* (Acacia, 2008), DVD.
[31] Simpson.

things.[32]

He remained admirably determined in the face of illness and impending death. Simpson recalled observing his rare determination as he taught himself how to walk again in a Memphis hospital. This powerful spirit was not only palpable to his close friends and family. When asked to define Jobs's legacy, biographer Walter Isaacson said, "It's his passion."[33]

The words that follow offer a deep insight into how death shaped the extraordinary life of Steve Jobs. "Remembering that you are going to die is the best way I know to avoid the trap of thinking you have something to lose," Jobs said in a commencement speech at Stanford in 2005, nearly a year after he was diagnosed with cancer.[34]

Innovation was a central theme in the life of Steve Jobs. Jobs's creativity was extraordinary, but he still remained grounded enough to understand that he would not be able to escape his own demise. Rather than be driven by a fruitless pursuit of immortality like other members of the Silicon Valley, Jobs soberly understood his relationship with the ultimate univer-

---

[32] Simpson.

[33] Ben Austen, "The Story of Steve Jobs: An Inspiration or a Cautionary Tale?" *WIRED*, July 23, 2012, accessed August 5, 2015, http://www.wired.com/2012/07/ff_stevejobs/.

[34] Kane and Fowler.

sal agreement. This allowed him to focus on what was important, bringing up his family and developing technological innovations that continue to transform our lives. His unique acceptance and understanding of death elevated him to live an extraordinary life.

# CHAPTER VII
## "American Immortal":
## Oliver Sacks and Ezekiel J. Emanuel

*"It matters not how a man dies, but how he lives. The act of dying is not of importance, it lasts so short a time."*

—SAMUEL JOHNSON

Oliver Sacks was a professor of neurology at the New York University School of Medicine. The world lost him in 2015. He is famous for numerous trailblazing books in the field. Looking back on his life, while nearing completion of an autobiography, he reflected, "I am grateful that I have experienced many things—some wonderful, some horrible—and that I have been able to write a dozen books, to receive innumerable letters from friends colleagues and readers, and to enjoy what Nathaniel Hawthorne called 'an intercourse with the world.'"[35]

Sacks was jubilant, staring down the specter of eighty. His father, who endured to the admirable age of ninety-four, frequently reminded his son that his eighties had been one of the very finest decades of his life. The younger Sacks marveled at the experience of making it to such an age. He said of his father, "He felt, as I begin to feel, not a shrinking but an enlargement of mental life and perspective. One has had a long experience of life, not only one's own life, but others', too. One has seen triumphs and tragedies, booms and busts, revolutions and wars, great achievements and deep ambiguities, too. One has seen grand theories rise, only to be toppled by stubborn facts. One is more conscious of transience and, perhaps, of beauty." Speaking of the milestone and what it means, Sacks continues: "At 80, one can take a long view and have a vivid, lived sense of history not possible at an earlier age. I can imagine, feel in my bones, what a century is like, which I could not do when I was 40 or 60. I do not think of old age as an ever grimmer time that one must somehow endure and make the best of, but

<hr>

[35] Oliver Sacks, "The Joy of Old Age. (No Kidding.)," *The New York Times*, July 6, 2013, accessed August 5, 2015, http://www.nytimes.com/2013/07/07/opinion/sunday/the-joy-of-old-age-no-kidding.html.

as a time of leisure and freedom, freed from the factitious urgencies of earlier days, free to explore whatever I wish, and to bind the thoughts and feelings of a lifetime together."[36]

He revealed to his readers how he had always correlated his age with atomic numbers; he was leaving the golden age of seventy-nine for mercury that was eighty on the atomic scale. Gold leads one to consider the symbolic durability and desirability, as well as the technological usefulness, of the precious metal, which is often extracted with the aid of mercury. Gold can be contrasted with the unique properties of mercury, a poisonous element that is fluid at room temperature and has the taint of unpredictability. Sacks has obviously deeply contemplated his mortality and the will to go on. He states: "Perhaps, with luck, I will make it, more or less intact, for another few years and be granted the liberty to continue to love and work, the two most important things, Freud insisted, in life."[37]

He observed that "at 80, the specter of dementia or stroke looms. A third of one's contemporaries are dead, and many more, with profound mental or physical damage, are trapped in a tragic and minimal exis-

---

[36] Sacks, "The Joy of Old Age. (No Kidding.)."
[37] Ibid.

tence. At 80 the marks of decay are all too visible. One's reactions are a little slower, names more frequently elude one, and one's energies must be husbanded, but even so, one may often feel full of energy and not at all 'old.'"[38] For those who have followed his story, this hope was not to be fulfilled but rather met with a sad turn of fate.

Tragically, Sacks was diagnosed with a terminal condition shortly after he turned eighty and wrote an eloquent op-ed piece about it in the *New York Times* on February 19, 2015. He was philosophical and resilient, saying: "Over the past few days, I have been able to see my life as from a great altitude, as a sort of landscape, and with a deepening sense of the connection of all its parts. This does not mean I am finished with life." He continues, somewhat defiantly: "On the contrary, I feel intensely alive, and I want and hope in the time that remains to deepen my friendships, to say farewell to those I love, to write more, to travel if I have the strength, to achieve new levels of understanding and insight.[39]

"I cannot pretend I am without fear. But my pre-

[38] Sacks, "The Joy of Old Age. (No Kidding.)."
[39] Oliver Sacks, "My Own Life: Oliver Sacks on Learning He Has Terminal Cancer."

dominant feeling is one of gratitude. I have loved and been loved; I have been given much and I have given something in return; I have read and traveled and thought and written. I have had an intercourse with the world, the special intercourse of writers and readers." He concludes his article with this enduring quote: "Above all, I have been a sentient being, a thinking animal, on the beautiful planet, and that in itself has been an enormous privilege and adventure."[40]

Many of Sacks's stances are questioned, though not directly, by Ezekiel J. Emanuel, a medical doctor who has held a number of positions in government since 2011. He currently heads the Department of Medical Ethics and Health Policy at the University of Pennsylvania. He opens his powerful essay in the *Atlantic*, "Why I Hope to Die at 75," with the statement: "Seventy-five. That's how long I want to live: 75 years."[41] He is not in favor of ending his life prematurely, but he is also deeply opposed to hanging on too long.

---

[40] Sacks, "My Own Life."
[41] Ezekiel J. Emanuel, "Why I Hope to Die at 75," *The Atlantic*, October 2014, accessed August 5, 2015, http://www.theatlantic.com/features/archive/2014/09/why-i-hope-to-die-at-75/379329/ .

He asserts that "death is a loss. It deprives us of experiences and milestones, of time spent with our spouse and children. In short, it deprives us of all the things we value." But he is quick to add that "a simple truth that many of us seem to resist" is that, like death, "living too long is also a loss." Interestingly, Emanuel has strong opinions on ending one's own life. He has "actively opposed legalizing euthanasia and physician-assisted suicide." He deftly explains that our quality of life and longevity have changed drastically in the last century.[42]

Emanuel makes this observation: "Americans seem to be obsessed with exercising, doing mental puzzles, consuming various juices and protein concoctions, sticking to strict diets, and popping vitamins and supplements, all in a valiant effort to cheat death and prolong life as long as possible. This has become so pervasive that it now defines a cultural type: what I call the American immortal."[43]

He mentions that in 1900 a newborn was expected to live for forty-seven years. But at the time of his article (2014), life expectancy was seventy-nine years. He continues to highlight the medical advances

---

[42] Emanuel.
[43] Ibid.

and other reasons that people are living longer. But the question that the author is asking is: what about the quality of the lives of those who are living longer? Are we living longer lives but diminishing the quality of our later years as we begin to decline?

Questions like these inspired a medical professor at Stanford, James F. Fried, to posit the theory of the "compression of morbidity." Emanuel contends that this line of thinking is central to the "American immortal," which he says boils down to the assertion that the longer one lives, the more that the extended portion of life is "spent in a state of decline." Therefore, that life lived in this extended state is increasingly diminished. This, the author contends, is fantasy. He concedes that senior citizens may be more able than they were fifty years ago, but he is quick to add: "But over recent decades, increases in longevity seem to have been accompanied by increases in disability—not decreases." He supports his position with facts gleaned from a study that health researcher Eileen Crimmins conducted by analyzing data from the Nation Health Interview Survey. Crimmins learned that Americans over the age of eighty were facing increasingly higher rates of functional limitation. After carefully studying the evidence, Crimmins concluded that there was a definite "increase in the life expectancy with disease and a decrease in the years without disease. The same is true for functioning loss, an increase in expected years unable to function."[44]

Crimmins and Emanuel are not alone in their views of the limitations that come with advanced aging. Their conclusions have been substantiated by a study of "healthy life expectancy" performed by the Health Metrics and Evaluation at the University of Washington and the Harvard School of Public Health, which found the opposite of a "compression of morbidity." They concluded that there was an "increase in the absolute number of years lost to disability as life expectancy rises."[45]

These findings can lead one to the uncomfortable conclusion that Crimmins came to after her study: rather than slowing the aging process, our efforts to prolong life are actually protracting the process of dying. Not only is this emotionally difficult for those who are impacted by the prolonged death of a loved one; it is also expensive for a society that spends so

---

[44] Emanuel.
[45] Ibid.

much money on the lackluster final couple of years of people's lives as they slowly crawl into the grave, hooked to fancy machines. Therefore, as the author points out, people are leading longer, yet more debilitated, lives.[46]

---

[46] Emanuel.

# CHAPTER VIII
# Facing Uncertainty
# Without Religion

*"Death is the cure for all diseases"*

—SIR THOMAS BROWNE

*"Death is not a period, but a comma in the story of life."*

—AMOS TRAVER

*"Life is pleasant. Death is peaceful. It's the transition that's troublesome."*

—ISAAC ASIMOV

Christopher Hitchens had a public battle with esophageal cancer, which he lost on December 15, 2012. Hitchens was a strong man who questioned the cliché of figuratively battling cancer in his book *Mortality*, which was culled mostly from a series of articles he wrote in *Vanity Fair* after he was diagnosed with the illness in June, 2010. In this "new world that lasted nineteen months," in the words of Hitchens's widow, Carol Blue, he himself was "living dyingly" as he described it.[47] The pages of *Mortality* are filled with his reflections and unflinching honesty. Hitchens describes the excruciating experience of trying to vanquish "this alien that can't want anything," because he was well aware of the cruel paradox that "if it kills me it dies but it seems very single-minded and set in its purpose." Contradictions like these have led many of those who share Hitchens's godless outlook to wonder why a deity would create a painful incubus that would enter a human being and steal the breath from their lungs, causing them and their family excruciating pain. This interesting point must have allowed Hitchens to hold on to his certainty that there is no God.[48]

Hitchens was a staunch atheist until the end, for which he was exalted and excoriated. His convictions enabled him to face death without a god, something that most humans throughout time have not done and that many people still find blasphemous. When

---

[47] Carol Blue, "Christopher Hitchens: An Impossible Act to Follow," *The Telegraph*, August 24, 2012, accessed August 5, 2015, http://www.telegraph.co.uk/culture/books/bookreviews/9480797/Christopher-Hitchens-an-impossible-act-to-follow.html.

[48] Christopher Hitchens, *Mortality*. (New York: Twelve, 2014), 97.

he was urged by members of many different faiths to convert in order to fling himself on the mercy of a god, he wryly noted that he would "sympathize afresh with the mighty Voltaire, who, when badgered on his deathbed and urged to renounce the devil, murmured that this was no time to be making enemies."[49] Hitchens certainly carried on the legacy of Voltaire, carrying over the wisdom gained from the age of reason and applying it to the modern day in his writing and public speaking. Although reason may be one of the mightiest tools that humankind has to make decisions in this confusing and ever-changing world, how does one reason with death?

Among some unfinished scrawls that Hitchens left behind, which were published in *Mortality*, is this quote from Saul Bellow: "Death is the dark backing that a mirror needs if we are able to see anything." This raises an interesting question: Death is an inevitability that we are all moving toward, but do we need to thoughtfully consider it to see reality more clearly?

The only insight I can offer as a writer who has felt his mortality is that there is the feeling that I am constantly slipping. There is never enough time to

---

[49] Hitchens, *Mortality*, 17.

read and write what I feel is important. To gaze into my own reflection of reality through words on a page, to make some sense of this life I lead in a puzzling and often depraved world—this is a large part of the introspective writer's life.

As his illness advanced, Hitchens feared losing his ability to write. With candor he explained that "without that ability, I feel sure in advance, my 'will to live' would be hugely attenuated. I often grandly say that writing is not just my living and my livelihood but my very life, and it's true." He concluded: "Almost like the threatened loss of my voice, which is currently being alleviated by some temporary injections into my vocal folds, I feel my personality and identity dissolving as I contemplate dead hands and the loss of the transmission belts that connect me to writing and thinking."[50]

The various trials, affectations, tribulations, occupations, and personal relationships that help us construct human identities are constantly at work throughout our lives. Personal identities are, at times, deeply mannered, and at others organic, constantly being woven into the tapestry of who we are as indi-

---

[50] Hitchens, *Mortality*, 70–71.

viduals. They are inextricable from the bodies that house these identities. Our bodies grow as we mature until we hit an apex (usually in heat of the summer of our lives, if looked at seasonally: in our late twenties or thirties), and there follows a decline that is more precipitous for some than others. Death is where the decline ends, but the awareness of the decline is much starker for those who are placed in the position to observe the decline with clarity, as Hitchens was, rather than those who are killed in an instant while in perfect health, or who meet the Reaper in a fog of dementia. For our entire lives we build a life, recognizing that it will inevitably slip away.

Hitchens reminds us that holding on too dearly can lead to hellish peril for the soon to be deceased and their loved ones. He offers the story of famous pragmatist, materialist, and fellow atheist, Sidney Hook. Hook was in Stanford, California, receiving some of the finest medical care available. He was able to endure numerous brushes with death that people in other generations or at other facilities would not have overcome. After one particularly nasty episode, from which he made a recovery, he made up his mind that he wished that he had not. As Hook wrote:

I lay at the point of death. A congestive heart failure was treated for diagnostic purposes by an angiogram that triggered a stroke. Violent and painful hiccups, uninterrupted for several days and nights, prevented the ingestion of food. My left side and one of my vocal cords became paralyzed. Some form of pleurisy set in, and I felt I was drowning in a sea of slime. In one of my lucid intervals during those days of agony, I asked my physician to discontinue all life-supporting services or show me how to do it.[51]

The physician would not grant him his wish and told Hook that "someday I would appreciate the un-wisdom of my request." But Hook was unmoved, living the rest of his life with the conviction that he should not continue to live, for three reasons: first, another stroke could compel him to relive all of the misery again. Second, the people he loved would be forced to endure the painful experience again. Third, the inordinate amount of medical care that was used on him could be better spent elsewhere. Hook said that he no longer wanted to be part of the legions of people who he lived with suffering on "mattress graves." His description of fellow terminally ill patients, near the ends of their lives, wasting away on

[51] Hitchens, *Mortality*, 64–65.

"mattress graves" is as chilling as it is evocative.[52]

Similarly, Hitchens was candid about the deep physical and mental suffering he faced during his final ordeal. Whether one is a devout believer or a staunch atheist there has to be some admiration for Hitchens's courage. He did not reach for a religious notion to lessen the burden, although a great deal of relief can be derived from faith. The notion that we are not facing the exit alone and that there is some sort of afterlife that awaits us offers succor to many. As a materialist, Hitchens believed that there was nothing beyond the curtain. Historically, there is little precedent for people facing death with no faith: throughout time, the vast majority of human beings have died with the consolation of their religious beliefs. Hitchens faced his death as he had lived: unconnected to religious grandeur.

---

[52] Hitchens, *Mortality*, 65.

# CHAPTER IX
# Beyond the Final Curtain:
# Reincarnation and the Afterlife

*"Death is the ornament of life."*

—JOSEPH CAMPBELL

*"Death is not the end, it is simply walking out of the physical form and into the spirit realm, which is our true home. It's going back home."*

—STEPHEN CHRISTOPHER

*"Of course you don't die. Nobody dies. Death doesn't exist. You only reach a new level of vision, a new realm of consciousness, a new unknown world."*

—HENRY MILLER

Although many religious texts give some version of what is beyond death, nobody can be sure. Books like *Proof of Heaven: A Neurosurgeon's Journey into the Afterlife* follow stories of people who "died" and claim to have drifted to the other side. But can we be certain that chemical processes in the brain are not creating elaborate hallucinations in these people's minds? This may be impossible to answer definitively. But for those who stay dead, who is to say where they have gone?

Most people reading this book have at least a vague idea of the Christian version of heaven and the pearly gates with Peter greeting them, weighing deeds, and so on. In this Christian version, hell is a hot and miserable place where you can hang out with people like Hitler, Stalin, and certain advertising executives. This all happens while a horned devil plots ways to make your stay in eternity as unpleasant as possible. Simply contemplating the prospect of this is enough to make one afraid to leave life. As a result, one would be constantly hoping that it is possible to qualify for entrance through the pearly gates, or at least an interim stay in purgatory.

To those with an outside perspective, many religious views of the afterlife can seem curious. The Tibetan view is a less publicized, and perhaps more nuanced. Interestingly, certain aspects of this view are shared with Western religions.

The Tibetan journey typically begins at the moment of death. Their concept of death and dying is very different from what is found in the West. At the time of death, the person is accompanied by a spiritual leader (a lama). This is not the moment to ask for acceptance from God, to talk about how great their life was, or to give any last rites. The lama is there to help the soul pass between worlds. When dying, the individual hopes to be integrated into the great light that illuminates all in order to escape the seemingly unending cycle of life and death, or reincarnation. In the Tibetan tradition, chakras are nexuses of energy that build from the base of the spine. In life, seekers participate in yoga, a complex set of spiritual and physical practices and other enriching experiences, trying to gain higher and higher chakra plateaus. As one ascends through the chakras, one gains greater levels of spiritual knowledge. The Tibetan tradition believes that the dying person follows each chakra in descending order, while reexamining their personal relationship to spiritual knowledge. This process is part of a greater process of rebirth into a higher earthly existence or, preferably, other more desirable spiritual realms. If the soul does not hold the light it plunges to the next chakra, where it must release the heaviness of its ego and give up on the illusion of plurality. It is in the next chakra that they must hold on to the image of the god they worshiped in their life to maintain the divinity before possibly being lowered yet again to the next chakra. Then there are many fascinating changes at the third chakra: the ego has solidified facing each of the five Buddhas (the four cardinal directions and one in the center) who are there to help the initiate and perhaps smash the ego if that is what is holding the soul back. This is before the level of fear of death, which occurs at the heart chakra. After this time one is filled with terrific terror; great powers tear apart the soul.[53]

Joseph Campbell likens the land of the knowledge holding deities, a place for those deities who have come to understand the cycles of life and death, to a college prom. This is a party that someone may find gruesome if they have not come to understand that death is not to be feared, but rather celebrated. They greet the outsider with banners made of "flayed human skin" and they are blowing trumpets made of thigh bones. They are still reveling in the thrill of the experience of death. They are draped in jewelry made

---

[53] *Mythos, Vol. 2: The Shaping of Our Mythic Tradition.*

of skulls, drinking blood from human craniums, while dancing. This representation goes back to the Hindu tradition and is represented by Kali, the goddess of time, change, power, and destruction. She is associated with death and is often portrayed wearing a garland of skulls.[54]

Then, as the spirit drops lower, there are deities who are screaming and gnashing their teeth. They have leonine faces and their purpose is to destroy the fear of death. At the following chakra the scene is similar to Christian themes, where bad deeds are weighed against good and punishments are doled out. Campbell asserts that "reincarnation is the counterpart, in the Orient, of purgatory in the West." He describes it as a chance to work out problems of the spirit in a different setting. If one cannot pass into the divine then the spiritual being is dropped even lower. This dark world is inhabited by those who still fear death and are bound to lust, ignorance, and malice. In this state the soul gets between mating couples, either human or animal, as it drops through the spiritual realm. If the soul is caught between an animal pair, it is reborn as an animal rather than a person. When the

[54] *Mythos, Vol. 2.*

eyes open after birth, the memories of the journey through the spirit world is forgotten.[55]

The Tibetan system of handling death becomes even more fascinating when one looks at recent discoveries by psychiatrists regarding the nature of past lives. Brian Weiss is a psychiatrist who uses hypnotism to help clients deal with past traumas. Many clients find it healing to reach back into events in their past, including in their childhoods, to work through and release stress. In the preface to *Many Lives, Many Masters*, Weiss describes his very traditional background as a young man who grew up in a "loving home" and knew by his sophomore year that he wanted to be a psychiatrist. He graduated magna cum laude from Columbia University before attending medical school at Yale. Weiss went on to a career as a distinguished professor at numerous venerable universities, but then everything changed for him. This transformation is reflected in the subtitle of his book: *The True Story of a Prominent Psychiatrist, His Young Patient, and the Past-Life Therapy That Changed Both Their Lives*. As Weiss notes: "Throughout history, humankind has been resistant to change and to the

[55] *Mythos, Vol. 2.*

acceptance of new ideas." His book challenges the way people view death.[56]

Weiss admits that he does not have a scientific answer to the amazing experiences he had with the client he refers to as "Catherine," the young woman who recounted past lives under hypnosis using a technique called hypnotic regression. The technique allows the psychologist to tap into trauma suffered early in a patient's life. Catherine's treatment with hypnotherapy was a last-ditch effort to treat her for severe phobias, anxiety, and panic attacks. Later, Weiss speculated that Catherine had reached back past her childhood. He guesses that while under hypnosis she accessed some trove of past-life experiences hiding deep within her subconscious, or was tapping into the collective unconscious, a theory central to the life's work of psychoanalyst Carl Jung. Weiss says that, at the time of the book's publication in 1988, scientists were starting to pursue "the mysteries of the mind, soul, the continuation of life after death, and the influence of our past-life experiences on our present behavior. Obviously, the ramifications are limitless, particu-

---

[56] Brian Weiss, *Many Lives, Many Masters: The True Story of a Prominent Psychiatrist, His Young Patient, and the Past-Life Therapy That Changed Both Their Lives* (New York: Touchstone, 1988).

larly in the fields of medicine, psychiatry, theology, and philosophy." He highlights the great advantages for a society to gain deeper insights into these matters.[57]

It is important to note that Catherine was a staunch Catholic and did not believe in reincarnation. This dispels the notion that her creative side may have taken over while under hypnosis and influenced her sessions with Dr. Weiss. Nor was Catherine an aberration; he has used hypnotic regression on many patients since his experience with her. These subsequent patients also reported events that went beyond their childhoods into the realm of past lives. Many people have reported these experiences to be healing, and in some cases cathartic.

Although many in the medical and psychiatric communities are dubious of such findings, Weiss is not alone in his practice or the revelations it has provided him. Dr. Wayne Dyer brought light to numerous near-death experiences that portended something greater, such as the one described in *Dying to Be Me* by Anita Moorjani. Medical evidence of her miraculous "return" from terminal cancer was reportedly con-

---

[57] Weiss, 11.

firmed in investigative interviews by her doctors.

Dr. Ian Stevenson has made some headway in a related field of study that has helped substantiate some of Weiss's findings. Since the 1960s Stevenson has documented the accounts of thousands of children between the ages of two and seven who have richly recounted memories from past lives. These accounts have been substantiated by documenting past-life events that the children could not have otherwise known about. For example, one boy who was born with a deformed hand insisted that his fingers were hacked away in his previous life. Stevenson was able to determine the village in which the boy had been assaulted and traveled there to document accounts. After investigating, he was convinced that the exact incident described had occurred.[58]

Stevenson's work was highly controversial. Regardless, he was compelled by these stories to the point that it became a life's obsession, convincing him that we are bound to a cycle of reincarnation. Though some of Stevenson's findings might be considered suspect, Weiss's reputation is solid, as he emerged from mainstream psychology and felt it his duty to expose

[58] Lisa Miller, "Remembrance of Lives Past," *New York Times*, August 27, 2010, http://www.nytimes.com/ 2010/ 08/29/ fashion/ 29PastLives.html?pagewanted=all&_r=2&.

what he had found for the betterment of society. He had little to gain professionally, and took a substantial risk in publishing *Many Lives, Many Masters* and pursuing his subsequent work in parapsychology. The facts are that this is a burgeoning field of study that has interested many trained professionals. Their investigations into uncanny phenomena indicate the reality of reincarnation, or at least a heightened sense of something beyond death.

Reincarnation is a concept that produces feelings of both reassurance and terror in many people. As a writer, I have long been spellbound by stories. Like many Westerners, growing up in a society where the Christian version of life and afterlife is pervasive in the culture, I have been surrounded by Christian tales and morality. When I learned about Eastern views, I listened to these versions of the afterlife with wonderment. What makes this even more intriguing is the accounts that professionals in the field of psychology have found, which indicate a rudimentary congruency, but not a full and irrefutable picture of the cycle of reincarnation. The rare place where science and spirituality meet is a realm we know little about but are becoming increasingly aware of. For me, this realm is a source of endless fascination. I have many more years of inquiry to spend. Ultimately, we may not find any definitive answers about death, which is curious since death can be considered the most definitive aspect of life.

# Conclusion

*"To die will be an awfully big adventure"*

—J. M. BARRIE

*"Seeing death as the end of life is like seeing the horizon as the end of the ocean."*

—DAVID SEARLS

As Gerda Erzberger, a character in Tom Rachman's novel *The Imperfectionists*, is dying of cancer, she points out: "You can't dread what you can't experience. The only death we experience is that of other people. That's as bad as it gets. And that's bad enough, surely."[59] Perhaps because of her state and limitations, this fictional character could not see the coming adventure. We can only speculate about what comes after life. Though we cannot say with certainty, when our time comes we may all know what caused

---

[59] Tom Rachman, *The Imperfectionists* (New York: Dial Press, 2011), 36.

Steve Jobs to utter his final words: "Oh wow. Oh wow. Oh wow."

Although no one can tell us what is beyond life, we have reason to believe that it is not transcendent, because an afterlife cannot be scientifically proven. But the key is that death is experienced by everyone on multiple levels: as an observer, as a person who has lost a loved one or a beloved pet, in brushes with death, and in recognizing the fact that death is inevitable for every living being (except perhaps Ray Kurzweil and other scions of Silicon Valley).

Therefore, it is important to gain a deeper under-standing of death from meditation on the meaning of it. The knowledge-seeking that you just engaged in by reading this book leads to a more open acceptance of the many meanings of death. You can achieve enlight-enment by simply spending time contemplating na-ture: the formation of clouds, the beauty of the forest, and the lifecycles of the beings that dwell within. Na-ture paradoxically embraces death while seeming also greater than death, and examining this concept can lead to increased acceptance. By exploring the depths of living as well as dying on this earth, we can gain a more profound philosophical understanding of the role of aging. This understanding can help us embrace the ultimate.

The seven-year-old who lost his beloved uncle and the seventeen-year-old who witnessed his grandfather's unique exit is still in the world, still staving off death, happy to share with you unique insights taken from difficult departures. For many, the understanding of what death is and acknowledging important aspects such as the finality of it for those who remain, is part of a constant process. As Leonardo da Vinci once said, "While I thought that I was learning how to live, I have been learning how to die."

We all know that one day we'll stagger off into eternity, but (we hope) not today. Doesn't that mean that we have to do the best we can with what we have, in this moment? The important truth that William Wallace captured is that "every man dies—not every man really lives." Death can be extremely difficult, but dying without truly living is perhaps the greatest of tragedies. Death is a profound lesson in truth: we grow to understand more about it from childhood until the day we must cross the mystic chasm and abandon the land of the living.

# Bibliography

Austen, Ben. "The Story of Steve Jobs: An Inspiration or a Cautionary Tale?" *WIRED*, July 23, 2012. Accessed August 5, 2015. http://www.wired.com/2012/07/ff_stevejobs/.

Blue, Carol. "Christopher Hitchens: An Impossible Act to Follow." *The Telegraph*, August 24, 2012. Accessed August 5, 2015. http://www.telegraph.co.uk/culture/books/bookreviews/9480797/Christopher-Hitchens-an-impossible-act-to-follow.html.

Cha, Ariana Eunjung. "How Silicon Valley's Billionaires Are Trying to Defy Death." *The Week*, May 3, 2015. Accessed August 20, 2015. http://theweek.com/articles/552604/how-silicon-valleys-billionaires-are-trying-defy-death.

Emanuel, Ezekiel J. "Why I Hope to Die at 75." *The Atlantic*, October 2014. Accessed August 5, 2015. http://www.theatlantic.com/features/archive/2014/09/why-i-hope-to-die-at-75/379329/.

Fowler, Yukari Iwatani and Geoffrey A. Kane. "Steven Paul Jobs, 1955-2011." *The Wall Street Journal*, October 6, 2011. Accessed August 5, 2015. http://www.wsj.com/articles/SB10001424052702304447804576410753210811910.

Gladwell, Malcolm. "The Tweaker." *The New Yorker*. Accessed August 5, 2015. http://www.newyorker.com/magazine/2011/11/14/the-tweaker.

Goldman, Andrew. "Ray Kurzweil Says We're Going to Live Forever." *The New York Times*, January 25, 2013. Accessed August 5, 2015. http://www.nytimes.com/2013/01/27/magazine/ray-kurzweil-says-were-going-to-live-forever.html.

Griffiths, Jay. *Wild: An Elemental Journey.* New York: Jeremy P. Tarcher/Penguin, 2006.

Hitchens, Christopher. *Mortality*. New York: Twelve, 2014.

Jones, Sam. "Steve Jobs's Last Words: 'Oh Wow. Oh Wow. Oh Wow.'" *The Guardian*, October 31, 2011. Accessed August 5, 2015. http://www.theguardian.com/technology/2011/oct/31/steve-jobs-last-words.

Krakauer, Jon. *Into the Wild*. New York: Anchor Books, 1996.

*Mythos, Vol. 2: The Shaping of Our Mythic Tradition*. Acacia, 2008. DVD.

O'Connor, Joe. "One of Dean S. Potter's Final Interviews: 'Every Death Has a Lesson.'" *National Post*. Accessed August 5, 2015. http://news.nationalpost.com/news/world/extreme-athlete-dean-s-potter-dies-during-failed-wingsuit-flight-in-yosemite-which-has-long-banned-the-practice.

Padmani. "Insects, Yoga, and Ayahuasca" in *Toward 2012: Perspectives on the Next Age*, edited by Daniel Pinchbeck and Ken Jordan. New York: Jeremy P. Tarcher/Penguin, 2008.

Rachman, Tom. *The Imperfectionists*. New York: Dial Press, 2011.

Rushe, Dominic. "Steve Jobs, Apple Co-Founder, Dies at 56." *The Guardian*, October 5, 2011. Accessed August 5, 2015. http://www.theguardian.com/technology/2011/oct/06/steve-jobs-apple-cofounder-dies.

Sacks, Oliver. "Oliver Sacks on Learning He Has Terminal Cancer." *The New York Times*, February 19, 2015. Accessed August 5, 2015. http://www.nytimes.com/2015/02/19/opinion/oliver-sacks-on-learning-he-has-terminal-cancer.html.

Sacks, Oliver. "The Joy of Old Age. (No Kidding.)." *The New York Times*, July 6, 2013. Accessed August 5, 2015. http://www.nytimes.com/2013/07/07/opinion/sunday/the-joy-of-old-age-no-kidding.html.

Salak, Kira. *Kira Salak*. Accessed November 6, 2015, http://www.kirasalak.com/.

Saulitis, Eva. "Cancer: Into the Wild Darkness." *The Week*. Accessed August 5, 2015. http://theweek.com/articles/446879/cancer-into-wild-darkness.

Simpson, Mona. "A Sister's Eulogy for Steve Jobs." *The New York Times*, October 30, 2011. Accessed August 5, 2015. http://www.nytimes.com/2011/10/30/opinion/mona-simpsons-eulogy-for-steve-jobs.html.

Weiss, Brian. *Many Lives, Many Masters: The True Story of a Prominent Psychiatrist, His Young Patient, and the Past-Life Therapy That Changed Both Their Lives*. New York: Touchstone , 1988.

# About the Author

The author grew up with a skeleton in his living room, and surrounded by other symbols of death. His unusual upbringing makes him uniquely qualified to serve as guide. As you join him in discovering more about death, you will find yourself enjoying a fuller life.

While living in New York City he attended both the famed Gotham Writers Workshop and the prestigious New York Writers Workshop where he was inspired to assiduously learn the craft of writing. He is a regular contributor to Can the Man (cantheman.com), an alternative media resource focused on social justice, and The Jovial Journey (thejovialjourney.com), a website dedicated to food, drink, and travel. He has written for *The Permaculture Research Institute* and *Uisio* among other prominent outlets.

He received a B.A. in World History from Manhattanville College in 2004 while minoring in World Religions. He attended the M.A. History program at Hunter College in Manhattan.

**REDSCORPION**
— PRESS —

Red Scorpion Press was formed in January 2016 with the hope of bettering the world in a small way through publishing. Our aim is to push boundaries and be an outlet for fresh voices and unique perspectives that entertain and inform.

Please visit us at www.redscorpionpress.com for our latest selection of books.

Made in the USA
Middletown, DE
19 June 2016